AN EVER-
PRESENT GOD

AN EVER-
PRESENT GOD

CARLESHA TAMIA HERNDON

Print information available on the last page.

Rev. date: 08/25/2020

To order additional copies of this book, contact:
Xlibris
844-714-8691
www.Xlibris.com
Orders@Xlibris.com
815064

Dedicated to all who need to be encouraged. Please keep the faith! Trust that God will see you throughout your life! He is with you in good things and when things don't seem so good. Be of good courage, for our God is a redeemer. There is hope and an assurance of victory and deliverance as long as you remain in Him.

CONTENTS

ACKNOWLEDGEMENTS

I would like to acknowledge God for allowing me to see His light, despite darkness and despair. I would like to acknowledge my mother, Josephine Herndon Fulton, whose memory and literary works kept my desire for writing going. I would like to acknowledge my family and loved ones, who I know believe in me, even when I struggle to see the gifts, I have embedded within me. God, be glorified and be lifted up through this book. Let people be encouraged and gravitate towards Jesus.

KEEP THE FAITH

Life can be a series of ups and downs. With different scenarios occurring daily, we often have to adjust and that can be frustrating. The ups of life bring happiness and contentment, yet the downs of life can stop us dead in our tracks. Sometimes, we are uncertain of how things will work out. During these times, it is important to keep the faith.

Keeping the faith means knowing that our God is faithful. It means having the confidence that God will make a way for us. Keeping the faith means upholding the promises of God in our lives.

Let us keep the faith when things do not look great. Keep the faith by understanding who God is to His people—He is Savior! God is our refuge, so when we are in trouble, we must run to Him—run to safety. Keep the faith when there are times of uncertainty. God is a sure thing; we can count on Him with everything concerning us.

REFLECT ON THIS: JAMES 1:2-4 (ESV)

Testing of Your Faith

² Count it all joy, my brothers, when you meet trials of various kinds, ³ for you know that the testing of your faith produces steadfastness. ⁴ And let steadfastness have its full effect, that you may be perfect and complete, lacking in nothing.

LEAN ON ME

There's a song from the late Bill Withers that says:

> *Lean on me, when you're not strong*
> *And I'll be your friend*
> *I'll help you carry on*
> *For it won't be long*
> *'Til I'm gonna need*
> *Somebody to lean on*

Just think, God always wants us to commune with Him! He calls us his friend and he will carry us when we are not able to stand on our own. He is with us through trials and tribulations.

There will be times when we cannot see our way out or through things, and believe it or not, it may be our own fault. Yet, our God's mercy and grace are what keeps us together.

We can come to him whenever and with whatever! When we don't have the answers (and believe that we will not have them), lean on God! Lean into our perfect Father! He is our saving grace!

REFLECT ON THIS:

"For I am the LORD your God, who upholds your right hand, Who says to you, 'Do not fear, I will help you.'

KEEP PRESSING

We have all experienced the lack of energy. Whether it is burnout, sleep deprivation, depression, grief, etc., we all have experienced a moment of depletion. This can happen physically, mentally and emotionally.

A way to conquer through feeling depleted is to keep pressing. When we press, we have to incorporate God into it. We cannot prosper without God. Pressing with God is seeking Him for guidance and then obeying what He says.

Pressing with God also means acknowledging that He has everything under control and we do not have control—relinquishing those things that are depleting us to Him is important. We must press on with God, knowing that we will be better with Him and therefore things will get better for us.

REFLECT ON THIS:

1 Peter 5:6-7 (NIV)

Humble yourselves, therefore, under God's mighty hand, that he may lift you up in due time. Cast all your anxiety on him because he cares for you.

DOWNCAST, BUT NOT DESTROYED

Have you ever been so down that it seemed as if you would not be able to ever feel joy again? Ever been so depressed that it seemed that you were taking a physical, mental and an emotional beating? Welp, it is not uncommon. That can be equated to being downcast. To be downcast is to be despondent or low in spirit. This feeling can often come as a result of a tumultuous event. It can also spring from past traumas that have not been resolved.

Nevertheless, being downcast, but not destroyed signifies that the low spirit is not here to say. Being down is temporary—it will not destroy you. In order to get a one up on it, consider taking it to God. Bring God into your situation.

Allow God to be the strength that you cannot seem to muster when you are downcast. With God, weapons form, but they will not prosper. God is bigger than anything! We will rise among that which seeks to weigh us down, so long as we keep God in the equation.

When feeling low in spirit, acknowledge the feeling. Then, take it a step further and acknowledge the author and finisher of our faith, our Lord and Savior. He will make it better!

REFLECT ON THIS:

2 Corinthians 4:7-11 (NKJV)

[7] But we have this treasure in earthen vessels, that the excellence of the power may be of God and not of us. [8] We are hard-pressed on every side, yet not crushed; we are perplexed, but not in despair; [9] persecuted, but not forsaken; struck down, but not destroyed— [10] always carrying about in the body the dying of the Lord Jesus, that the life of Jesus also may be manifested in our body. [11] For we who live are always delivered to death for Jesus' sake, that the life of Jesus also may be manifested in our mortal flesh.

THE SENSE-MAKER

There will be times when things will not make sense. In times of uncertainty, we often want to try to solve the mysteries on our own. We often try to figure things out for ourselves. It is during these times that we should lean into our God. He has the answers to all that concerns us. God is the sense-maker; He is the constant in our world of variables.

Drawing near to his guidance is a comforting experience. It is also a humbling and obedient act. God loves when we come to Him. He is our confidant and cares for us deeply. In God, there is comfort, love, tranquility, and rest.

Resting in God means we are trusting Him. He is a faithful God who wants what is best for us. There will be occurrences in our daily life that will require God. They are not purposed for us to handle. Instead, they are purposed so that we might look to the sense-maker!

In all that does not make sense, in all of the equations of life that do not add up, trust God! Let God into your confusion. Replace that confusion with comfort and relief. God is waiting!

REFLECT ON THIS:

1 Corinthians 14:33 New International Version (NIV)

³³ For God is not a God of disorder but of peace—as in all the congregations of the Lord's people.

LOVE LIFTED ME

Who do you turn to when you need love? Is it your relative, your significant other, or do you just feel too reserved to admit you need love at all?

When love is needed, there is someone who loves so much that it is often incomprehensible! That someone is God! God loves with the kind of love that cannot lose! It is unfiltered, undying love.

There have been times where love has not been something to gravitate towards. There have been disappointing occurrences that made us feel as though love is far and few. God's love is the cure for that. His love LIFTS us up. Love should be pure and joyous. It should nurture your entire being. We can count on God's love to be just that.

Seek His love above any other person's love. His love LIFTS us out of despair, out of frustration and out of hate. His love can help you to smile again. God's love LIFTs us out of the darkness and into His marvelous light!!

REFLECT ON THIS:

1 John 4:9-16 New International Version (NIV)

⁹ This is how God showed his love among us: He sent his one and only Son into the world that we might live through him. ¹⁰ This is love: not that we loved God, but that he loved us and sent his Son as an atoning sacrifice for our sins. ¹¹ Dear friends, since God so loved us, we also ought to love one another. ¹² No one has ever seen God; but if we love one another, God lives in us and his love is made complete in us.

¹³ This is how we know that we live in him and he in us: He has given us of his Spirit. ¹⁴ And we have seen and testify that the Father has sent his Son to be the Savior of the world. ¹⁵ If anyone acknowledges that Jesus is the Son of God, God lives in them and they in God. ¹⁶ And so we know and rely on the love God has for us.

God is love. Whoever lives in love lives in God, and God in them.

HIS LOVE SAVED THE DAY

God is a great father! He often saves us from dangers seen and unseen. His favor, His care and His providence are not lost on any of His children. When we are in a bind, God comes through for us. He is consistently there for us because He loves us. His love saves the day! We could be having the worst of days and God can turn it around.

He sends His love in many ways. It may be as a subtle as a hug from someone, a call or text from someone to uplift you when they know nothing of the trials and tribulations in your life. God sends love in the form of the Holy Spirit. The Holy Spirit helps us to stay in tune with God, even though we are surrounded by worldly desires.

God's love permeates through our problems. His love allows us to look past our pain and see what He wants for us and how He may want to use us to help others. God's love saves us from sin, from disastrous times and from worries. We should seek Him in all our ways!

REFLECT ON THIS:

Ephesians 2:1-4 (GW)

¹You were once dead because of your failures and sins. ² You followed the ways of this present world and its spiritual ruler. This ruler continues to work in people who refuse to obey God. ³ All of us once lived among these people, and followed the desires of our corrupt nature. We did what our corrupt desires and thoughts wanted us to do. So, because of our nature, we deserved God's anger just like everyone else. ⁴ But God is rich in mercy because of his great love for us.

EXALTING GOD OVER ANXIETY

When anxious, there is the loss of control. There's an awareness that things are spiraling out of one's control and there is nothing that can be done, but to ride it out, take deep breaths and try to get through it. Anxiety is described as a feeling of nervousness, worry, and/or uneasiness. Anxiety, although an overwhelming feeling/experience, is no match for God's goodness.

God is in control of everything! He knows every single detail of our lives. Exalting God over anxiety is recognizing God's faithfulness. Exalting God over anxiety relinquishes the stronghold anxiety seemingly has on us and giving that power to God.

When we exalt God, we reverence Him. We lift up God so that He may receive glory. Exalting God allows us to let go of what seemingly holds us hostage. We then are able to accept God's freedom, grace and thereby relief is on the way!

Exalt God over anxiety! Give Him glory and release anxiety!

REFLECT ON THIS:

Romans 8:26-28 (NIV)

26 In the same way, the Spirit helps us in our weakness. We do not know what we ought to pray for, but the Spirit himself intercedes for us through wordless groans. ²⁷ *And he who searches our hearts knows the mind of the Spirit, because the Spirit intercedes for God's people in accordance with the will of God.* ²⁸ *And we know that in all things God works for the good of those who love him, who have been called according to his purpose.*

DELIVERANCE

God's deliverance is an amazing gift! It is something that is not soon forgotten. God's deliverance is equated to being rescued by a lifeguard. We are in danger of perishing, and God comes in and rescues us!

Thinking about God's deliverance, we should reflect on how we do not deserve it. We have made countless mistakes and we are definitely without sin. Yet, God knows this and loves and delivers us anyhow! Whew! What a great God He is!

If ever you are in a mood where you feel like you need more, like what you have and who you are just are not enough, think about God's deliverance. His love and rescuing us goes back to Calvary, where His only Son, Jesus was slain. Jesus was slain for our deliverance! What more could we want or need!? If anything, we should strive to seek out and do what God requires of us!

God's deliverance should not bring disappointment, but delight! Be mindful that God's deliverance is a gift that cannot be repaid in the same manner by any person on earth! ONLY GOD could do it!

REFLECT ON THIS:

Galatians 5:1 (NIV)

It is for freedom that Christ has set us free. Stand firm, then, and do not let yourselves be burdened again by a yoke of slavery.

REFUGE

Safety is something we all want to feel. We do not want to live life in fear. We all would like to have a sense of security daily. While life is full of possibilities and we do not have the ability to shield ourselves from all harm or danger, we can look to God, who is our Savior. God is our refuge! We can go to Him and there He is, shielding us from dangers seen and unseen.

God is our strong tower and provider! His love and protection allow us to freely go about our day. He is with us daily, going before us to ensure we are covered. Having refuge in God gives us the courage to go out and be who He has called us to be. The fear subsides when we place God in front of it and totally trust Him to be our refuge, our strong tower and our way-maker!

In times of trouble, we must trust God to bring us through the dangers and toils. Bonus: the dangers we are in could be repercussions of our disobedience and God will STILL be our refuge!

REFLECT ON THIS:

Psalm 71:3 (NIV)

³ Be my rock of refuge, to which I can always go; give the command to save me, for you are my rock and my fortress.

HOLY SPIRIT= HELPMATE

The Holy Spirit is an entity of God that is used to help us along our daily walk with God. The Holy Spirit is our helpmate. It is God's guidance for us. We should continuously seek the Holy Spirit where it concerns our daily lives. The Holy Spirit intercedes for us. The Holy Spirit prays the prayers we cannot pray The Holy Spirit instills in us God's will and desire for us.

The Holy Spirit helps us daily. The Holy Spirit is our helper, aligning us up with God's word. When the Holy Spirit helps us, it is for our good. Even when we want to do our own thing, God sends the Holy Spirit to get us in line and to keep us in His will. Our helpmate knows our weaknesses and our heart. After all, the Holy Spirit is of God and God knows all!

When things become too difficult for us to handle, we should run to our helpmate—the Holy Spirit. When we think we know it all, even then, lean into our helpmate to be sure we are doing what God wants us to do!

REFLECT ON THIS:

John 14:26 (NIV)

26 But the Advocate, the Holy Spirit, whom the Father will send in my name, will teach you all things and will remind you of everything I have said to you.

GET BACK UP AGAIN

Sometimes, in this life, there will be weary days. There will be days where we will feel down, beat up, and down for the count. These days are not easy. These days are not always the brightest. Please do not think that in this life we will not have cloudy days.

We all will come across, and with God's help, come through some hard times. Take courage! Be encouraged that God will allow us to be redeemed. He can turn the situations we are in around. While we have been down, we have the ability to get back up again! We have everything already embedded in us to get back up and keep on going!

God has given us a sound mind! He has given us a conquering spirit! Because God is victorious, as His children so are we! Satan is defeated every time we get back up again! Problems are miniscule every time we say yes to God to get us through them! Trouble don't last always. God does! God's love and kindheartedness lasts always! With Him, we always win! Keep saying yes to God!

Keep getting up! Keep showing up! Keep pressing forward! God is not done with us! We cannot give up! We must not throw in the towel! Get back up again! Give it all over to God and watch Him show up and show out on our behalf!

REFLECT ON THIS:

Proverbs 24:16 (ESV)

For the righteous falls seven times and rises again, but the wicked stumble in times of calamity.

OK GOD, NOW WHAT?

When we get to a place where we feel like we are on top of all that God has called us to do, do we often feel like, ok, now what? Or, when so much has happened in our lives, and it all seems like it is tumbling down on our heads, do we ask God, ok now what?

This question can be a start to something very interesting. If you feel like you have done enough and feel like you have done all that God has called you to do, be mindful that the work is never done! There is always room to be better and to do more. There are always going to be souls that need to be won and bought to Christ while we are here on earth.

If you feel overwhelmed and think, what more can happen, be mindful that God is still with you and you are afforded peace. God designed us to call on Him for our refuge. God wants us to continually rely on Him for love and sustenance. While asking God what more are you going to have to endure, be mindful that your endurance and perseverance comes from the tests and trials of life. Consider that God is trying to show you just how strong HE is and how strong you are, or will be, when you acknowledge Him in and through it all!

Ultimately, we should look for God in our process. We should want to see how our Father is going to handle all that concerns us. We should stay in His presence, seeking Him for next steps, be it we want to do more for His kingdom, or if we just need His guidance and glory to fall upon us.

REFLECT ON THIS:

Isaiah 30:21 (NIV)

Whether you turn to the right or to the left, your ears will hear a voice behind you, saying, "This is the way; walk in it."

WHO CAN I RUN TO?

When the trials of life are getting the best of us and we want to scream and run away from it all, where should we go? Often, we cannot even go to the people who we deem are our closest and most beloved because it just does not seem like there will be any relief or solace in going to them. Sometimes, we want someone who will completely and totally understand what we are facing and have the solution for our problems.

That person is our Lord and Savior. God sees everything we go through. Quite frankly, He knows every detail, every mishap, every joy, every sorrow, and every confusing time we will face. God is the person we should be running to for our help. He is the only one who has a definite resolve for our dilemma.

When we run to God, we can expect love. His love knows no bounds.

When we run to God, we can expect peace. His peace is soothing and unlike anything else.

When we run to God, we can expect mercy and support. God wants us to come to Him. God wants to extend His helping hand and do what He already knows we cannot do without Him.

So, flee to safety! Run to God when the going gets tough. Whenever we say to ourselves and others that something is too much, we should have the same ability to say who can make it all better—God!

REFLECT ON THIS:

Exodus 3:7 (NIV)

[7] The LORD said, "I have indeed seen the misery of my people in Egypt. I have heard them crying out because of their slave drivers, and I am concerned about their suffering."

NEVER ALONE

How is it possible to feel alone, even when we may be surrounded by people? What is the best way to cope with loneliness?

Sometimes, we feel left out of the loop. Sometimes, we may even feel like nobody is concerned about us. When we have these feelings on loneliness, self-loathing, and just feel like we do not matter, we should put our minds, our hearts and our focus on Jesus. Go down memory lane—think about all the times God allowed us happiness, blessings and pure joy. Think about the sacrifice of Jesus Christ. Take a moment to think about it. We can even take the time to read and understand it in God's word. God allowed Jesus to come here on earth to live and die for our sins. He gave HIS ONLY begotten son so that we can live on earth today.

The sacrificial lamb that is Jesus Christ is more than enough proof that we matter to God. It is proof that we have never been alone and will never be alone. God is always with us! The resurrection of Jesus is an example of God's continuous love and understanding of what we need while we are here on earth.

Be reminded that we are never alone. We are God's children, children that are nurtured, valued and loved with the love that always wins!

REFLECT ON THIS:

Hebrews 13:5-6 (NIV)

⁵ Keep your lives free from the love of money and be content with what you have, because God has said, "Never will I leave you; never will I forsake you." ⁶ So we say with confidence, "The Lord is my helper; I will not be afraid. What can mere mortals do to me?"

WAYMAKER

There have been times where we have seemed all hope was lost. There have been times where we could not do something on our own. There have been challenges in this life and we had no clue as to how we would recover from them.

God has been with us every step of the way. When we felt as if there was no hope for us, God was there, providing a clear path for us. When we could not do something on our own, God made sure we had the ability to get it done, be it through giving us strength or sending people to us to bring us through that rough patch. The challenges of our lives are not lost on God. He is our waymaker! He is the truth and the light in hopeless and dark situations.

God covers His children with His faithful love and steadfastness. He is sovereign—there is nothing and nobody like our God! He can wash away our sins. He can forgive us time after time. He can allow people into our lives that will help us to do better and to be better.

God has given us unique gifts that help us to get through this life. His ways are not like ours because He knows full well every need, every matter, every circumstance and every outcome. Let our God make ways that no person can! Let us permit Him into our lives daily to permeate every situation we may be faced with! He is an awesome provider and certainly the most reliable waymaker we can ever encounter!

REFLECT ON THIS:

Joshua 21:45 (NIV)

[45] *Not one of all the Lord's good promises to Israel failed; every one was fulfilled.*

SUFFICIENT GRACE

God's grace is something so amazing to behold. It is one of the best gifts from our Father. His grace is an allowance—it gives us the right to be ourselves. His grace allows us to conquer things that would otherwise destroy us.

When thinking of grace, we should think of understanding, admittance, solitude, having the ability to do more that our minds can comprehend.

God's grace is efficient. In other words, it is enough! It works for our good days. Moreover, we appreciate it even more on those not so good days. When times are so burdening, God's grace is an extension of His love for us. Grace is God's consent for us to sit with Him, to have a breath of fresh air. Grace is just as good as a good night's rest. In God's sufficient grace, there are no worries. Instead, the things we would usually worry about are replaced with an absoluteness that only our Father can bring upon us.

Another good thing about grace is that it comes about at a time where we are most vulnerable. God extends grace when we have seemingly exhausted all options and are at our wick's end. In comes God! Here he is, showing us grace and reminding us that all is well, as long as we stay in Him. What an honor it is to have a God that loves us so much that even in weakness, His grace covers all that we stand in need of!

REFLECT ON THIS:

2 Corinthians 12:9 (ESV)

⁹ But he said to me, "My grace is sufficient for you, for my power is made perfect in weakness." Therefore I will boast all the more gladly about my weaknesses, so that Christ's power may rest on me.

HOLDING ONTO HIS GRACE

We all have fallen short. We all have missed the mark. No one on this earth is perfect. We all need God's grace in our lives. Recognizing this is pivotal to keeping His grace near and dear to us.

When we fall short and need forgiveness from God, we should hold onto His saving grace. Holding onto God's grace means we acknowledge that we need it consistently in our lives. We are often inconsistent when we base our daily dealings on how we feel. However, if we considered the grace of God and His allowance of love, happiness and mercy in our lives then we will begin to adapt to living a life where we do not want to let go of all that God has for us.

Hold onto God's grace when things seem to spiral out of control.

Hold onto God's grace as you maneuver through grief.

Hold onto God's grace when there is uncertainty and mental anguish.

Hold onto God's grace, resting in the promises He has made that cannot be denied. Holding onto God's grace is holding onto security and resulting in love and freedom, mentally, physically and emotionally.

REFLECT ON THIS:

Psalm 55:19 (NIV)

[19] *God, who is enthroned from of old, who does not change—he will hear them and humble them, because they have no fear of God.*

BETTER DAYS

As we all go through life, there will be days where we do not feel great. There will be times of depletion, be it mental depletion, emotional exhaustion, or physical depletion. When we feel defeated and there is no energy left to deal with the strife of this world, we often want to escape it all. We wonder, when will there be relief?

Don't fret! Better days are coming! There will be better days ahead for us. While God did not promise us all great and cheerful times, He does promise that we will have better days with Him in the future.

Our God knows of every circumstance and is prepared to deliver us from each circumstance. We are better with our God! We can live a more joyous, peaceful, and content life when we know that God is our greatest support system. Because of the support of our King, we will have better days come our way!

Better days are something to look forward to, especially when we are going through what seems to be hellish times. Better days are a result of our faith and obedience in our Lord. Relinquish your anguish and exchange it for better—better with our God!

REFLECT ON THIS:

Zephaniah 3:17 (NIV)

The LORD your God is with you, the Mighty Warrior who saves. He will take great delight in you; in his love he will no longer rebuke you, but will rejoice over you with singing.

OH, TO BE KEPT!

When there are the deep, dark places where there seems to be nobody to pull you through, you should be comforted in knowing that our God is still with us! He keeps us daily! As long as we have breath in our bodies, God is alongside us, keeping us through every trial. He keeps on making ways for us!

Oh, to be kept! It is such a privilege! We are getting blessed beyond what we deserve. We are being blessed beyond what we can measure. To be kept by God is significant to His children, having an inkling of all of the mess we have, all of the flaws that come with us, and the times where we are disobedient—we know we are being kept when we get another chance at life.

Oh, to be kept by our God! He keeps on giving us chances to do and be better daily. When we are kept by God, we must recognize that we are being kept by Him for a reason. We are being kept by God to live out our purpose and finish what He has given us as our assignment while we are here on earth.

As we go through our lives, let us always grasp onto the fact that God is keeping us! We should desire to be kept by the King!

REFLECT ON THIS:

2 Thessalonians 3:3 (NIV)

But the Lord is faithful, and he will strengthen you and protect you from the evil one.

WHO YOU ARE AND WHOSE YOU ARE

Our identity in Christ Jesus is important to obtain so that we will not easily be swayed by temptation. When we know who we are and whose we are, we understand the promises of God. We understand what God is teaching us and we know that there is a divine purpose. When we know who we are, we acknowledge that our live in Christ is one where nobody should be able to break it. The bond between us and our Lord should solidify whose we are. We are loyal to our Father. We belong to our God.

Knowing who we are and whose we are is reminiscent of being heirs of salvation! The fact that Jesus came here on earth, lived, taught, healed and prayed amongst people, and sacrificed His life (obediently) so that we all might have life is the epitome of truly understanding who we are and whose we are!

Whenever you start to second guess things, hang onto the fact that God loves you, undeniably and nothing can change that. Hang onto the fact that with God everything is going to be alright! Hang onto the fact that you belong to God and in that belonging lies security, love and an amazing future! Know who you are! Remember whose you are! Never lose sight of your connection with God!

REFLECT ON THIS:

Galatians 4:7 (NIV)

So you are no longer a slave, but God's child; and since you are his child, God has made you also an heir.

BABY STEPS

In this life, we do not have all the answers. We often have to wade through unchartered territory. It is equivalent to a child learning to walk for the first time. It is foreign, but as the child takes small steps and keeps trying every day, they eventually are able to walk. God allows us the same experience as adults. He is like the parent at the other end, arms outstretched, waiting for us to take our baby steps to him.

When we take those baby steps toward God, not knowing what is ahead, we are putting our full trust in Him. We say, by each step that we take, that God, lead the way! By each step, we show Him that He is in control and we are stepping closer to Him for our refuge.

Baby steps are indicators of our faith. Inching our way to our Father is a reminder that He is our provider. It is a reminder that He knows what is best for us. By taking these baby steps, we are able to experience the goodness that comes from trusting Him. Our fears are compensated with God's direction, His love and His mercy!

REFLECT ON THIS:

Psalm 103:13 (NIV)

As a father has compassion on his children, so the LORD has compassion on those who fear him.

AN OPEN RELATIONSHIP

When we are in a relationship with our father, there is a sense of freedom that comes with it. This relationship is open—allowing for direct access daily, at any hour, minute or second. We do not have limitations on our access to our God!

Our God welcomes an open relationship with us. He desires us to openly express ourselves to Him, bringing Him everything that concerns us. Having this kind of relationship should be a comfort to all of His children. An open relationship with God means no difficulty getting through to Him and also no difficulty for Him to get through to us.

Having an open relationship with the Lord means we can communicate as frequent as we need to. We can come to Him as authentically and as raw as we can. Nothing is too hard, to small, too big or too much for our Father. Having an open relationship with God is an amazing experience, for it allows for God's light to shine on our lives and it progresses our purpose and His will!

REFLECT ON THIS:

Deuteronomy 7:9 (NIV)

Know therefore that the LORD your God is God; he is the faithful God, keeping his covenant of love to a thousand generations of those who love him and keep his commandments.

GOD'S GUARANTEE

Did you know that God has guaranteed that we can rely on Him? There are several instances in His word that leads His children to believe that He is trustworthy. God guarantees us His love, His righteousness, His forgiveness and that His will is what is most advantageous for us.

God guarantees His love for us through His only Son Jesus. Jesus is our gateway to God. Jesus is the epitome of love. It was Jesus who gave His life so that we might have an everlasting relationship with God the Father. God guarantees us His righteousness by giving us examples of how to live right. He allowed Paul to display and teach righteousness to His people. God guarantees His forgiveness every single time that we repent for our wrongdoings. God extends mercy when we turn from our wrongness and back to his loving kindness. Ultimately, God's will for us is a guarantee that is unlike no other. He knows all that we are and all that we will face and has a goal for each of us. This guarantee is one that results in long-lasting love, peace, joy, reconciliation, and life with our Lord.

God's guarantee for us to be more with Him cannot be overturned. He has the final say as it pertains to our lives. God's guarantee should be our security!

REFLECT ON THIS:

Ephesians 1:13-14 (NIV)

And you also were included in Christ when you heard the message of truth, the gospel of your salvation. When you believed, you were marked in him with a seal, the promised Holy Spirit, who is a deposit guaranteeing our inheritance until the redemption of those who are God's possession—to the praise of his glory.

BE GRATEFUL

In this life we have many things we can criticize. There are many things that, in our eyes, could be different, or dare we say, better. Nevertheless, God's gift of life is something to be cherished. We should always acknowledge the many good things that God has done. We should also acknowledge the many dangerous things God has spared us from—His deliverance is a delight!

God's grace and mercy are gifts that we can never repay Him for, so we should be grateful to Him for His allowance of both grace and mercy. Furthermore, it would be wise, and bring our Father great joy, to extend grace and mercy to our fellow brothers and sisters. That extension is also a form of gratitude (paying it forward).

When times are hard, be grateful for the times that we were allotted goodness and ease. When things are confusion, be grateful and mindful of our powerful Lord and Savior who looks out for us and knows what we do not know. When hate is boiling up in our minds, our hearts and bodies, think of the calmness and the love that God shows to us and we should replace hatred with understanding and love. Be grateful for each blessing and each lesson as you journey through life. Through God's constant love, gratitude should be effortless to return to Him.

REFLECT ON THIS:

Psalm 7:17 (NIV)

I will give thanks to the Lord because of his righteousness; I will sing the praises of the name of the Lord Most High.

TRIED AND TRUE

It is interesting that often we have to try something for ourselves in order to determine whether or not it is authentically good. We may even need to see/hear something for ourselves to believe it to be true. Even more interesting is that the goodness of God is not always exempt from this mindset. Plenty of us, as believers, want to experience God in a way that is relative to what we are going through. We want to have a testimony. We want to be able to say, oh, yeah, God does work. Once we experience this testimony, which God has no problem to prove Himself to us and to nonbelievers alike, it becomes a tried and true ordeal.

We begin to take God's ways seriously. We have an instance where God worked something out—He showed us exactly who He is and what He is capable of in our lives. Having a tried and true moment means that we can attest to our Lord's faithfulness. Therefore, we can enlighten and even encourage someone else of God's good ways. As we think of this, let us be mindful that God has already proven Himself to be tried and true. Other ways in which God can be found to be tried and true are in His word! Tap into His word and it will not be long before there's a discovery of one's own tried and true moment. After all, aligning up with God's word equates to aligning up with His will for our lives.

REFLECT ON THIS:

Psalm 18:30 (NLT)

God's way is perfect. All the LORD's promises prove true. He is a shield for all who look to him for protection.

TOTAL ACCESS

Have you ever thought of how God has no limits? He has nothing or no one restricting Him for doing what He wants to do. What about How His love is—how it knows no bounds and is unconditional? These thoughts should allow God's children to appreciate Him for the wonderful Father that He truly is to us. God has provided us access both on earth and in heaven!

Nothing separates us from Him! We have total access to our King! He welcomes us to come to Him, to access His excellence and seek His wisdom as it pertains to our life's journey. A clear sign that we have total access to God is the fact that we can freely worship, pray, praise and seek Him. He does not force us, and we have the ability to have a relationship with Him that the world did not give, therefore the world cannot take it away.

Total access to God is a privilege. When we recognize all that God is and our worth to our Lord, we should exalt God! Take advantage of the completeness of God. Take advantage of the total access we have to God the Father because of the sacrifice of His only Son, Jesus! There is a cost that we did not pay for this access and we ought not take it for granted!

REFLECT ON THIS:

Hebrews 4:16 (NLT)

So let us come boldly to the throne of our gracious God. There we will receive his mercy, and we will find grace to help us when we need it most.

GOD OVER GRIEF

Losing a loved one is not easy on us. As human beings, we go through gut-wrenching pain when someone we love and cherish passes away. Then grief sinks into us. It grips us tightly, seemingly surrounding us. Often, it blinds us, shutting down our minds, our hearts and even our bodies.

We go through the stages of grief: 1. Denial- we cannot wrap our minds around what has happened. 2. Anger- we are anguished and frustrated with ourselves and others about the loss of our loved ones. 3. Bargaining- we wish we could trade places, or offer up something to bring our loved one back. 4. Depression- things become dark, dank, mundane, empty, careless, time seemingly stops; there's a sense of blankness and we often want to be alone. 5. Acceptance- we slowly understand that our loved one is not returning and we are left with trying to move on with our lives.

While these stages come and go, in whatever order they want, we must be mindful that God is with us. He hears our groan (in fact, he pities every groan). He is with us when we cannot understand. He is with us when we think we are alone. He is with us in our anger (and He can handle it). He is the light that glimmers in the darkness of depression. He is with us every step of the way, nurturing and healing us. God is greater than our grievances! He is greater than grief! God is life! He is the constant that keeps us grounded and rooted as we navigate through life, while here on earth. He is the prize and the privilege that awaits us when we get to our heavenly homes! Grief is temporary, but God is everlasting!

REFLECT ON THIS:

Isaiah 25:8 (NIV)

He will swallow up death forever. The Sovereign LORD will wipe away the tears from all faces; he will remove the disgrace of his people from all the earth. The LORD has spoken.

GLORIFYING GOD

Our God has bestowed many blessings upon us. He is a glorious Father. It should be a no-brainer to give God glory and honor for all that He is to us! To glorify God is to recognize that He is our first love. Glorifying God is realizing that He is the only One who can save us from ourselves and others. To glorify our Father is simply acknowledging that He is our All in All!

When we glorify God, sometimes it will be just because. Other times, it will be as we are going through one of life's many trials. Then there will be the glorification of a triumph—after God has delivered us and has shown Himself mighty in our lives. No matter the circumstance, we should give God glory every chance we can. The mere fact that tomorrow is not promised and we are living today is a reason to give God glory!

There are many reasons to glorify God. He shows us countless times in His word how mighty He is and the power that He has. He shows up for us daily, providing gifts of grace and mercy that we surely do not deserve. He allows us access to Him 24/7, so there's not a time He is not available for us to shower Him with love, come to Him for guidance and to just rest on Him. Glorify God in your strengths, in your weaknesses, in your good days and not so good days. If He deemed us worth saving (from our own deplorable sins), we owe Him all glory and honor!

REFLECT ON THIS:

1 Corinthians 10:31 (NIV)

So whether you eat or drink or whatever you do, do it all for the glory of God.

LIGHT AT THE END OF THE TUNNEL

Darkness is like confusion. Nothing can be seen. Nothing is clear. There is the feeling that you will never see the light of day again. With darkness, there is a gloomy and eerie feeling. The opposite of darkness is light, where there is clarity, clearness, and a sense of warmth and awareness.

The light at the end of the tunnel is a symbolism of hope. It is like a diamond in the rough. Once you see the light, there's an instant gratification that comes with it. Think about life without Christ. There is no clear direction. Often times, it feels like you are winging it, and there is no guidance. There also seems to be countless mistakes and unwanted/unnecessary pain. Now, think about life with Christ. It is like seeing a light at the end of a long, dark tunnel. With God, there is gratitude. With Christ there is a sense of belonging. With Christ we become more aware, we have clearer guidance, and have the Holy Spirit as a companion, helping us to emotionally, spiritually and physically maneuver through the roads of life.

The light at the end of the tunnel is our hope. As believers in Christ, we set our hope and put our trust in the One who is able to keep us from falling! Remember that God is our guiding light, encouraging us to be the salt and light on the earth!

REFLECT ON THIS:

1 John 1:5 (NLT)

This is the message we heard from Jesus and now declare to you: God is light, and there is no darkness in him at all.

FINAL WORDS

This devotional was created to offer solace, hope, love, and strength in Christ. This book is a reminder that God loves us totally, recklessly and we have the ability to stay grounded in Him through His love and His desire for us to be with Him forever. To know an ever-present God is to accept that we are winners, we are victorious because we serve a God who is all-knowing and all-powerful! Our God is awesome and always wins! Remember to cast everything aside and put Him first!

CPSIA information can be obtained
at www.ICGtesting.com
Printed in the USA
BVHW030021141020
590973BV00001B/79